P9-CAU-162

Hard Work

A Day with Police Officers

By Jan Kottke

Welcome Books

SCHOLASTIC INC.
New York Toronto London Auckland Sydney
Mexico City New Delhi Hong Kong Buenos Aires

Photo Credits: Cover, p. 5, 7, 9, 13, 17, 21 by Thaddeus Harden;
p. 11 © FPG; p. 15, 19 © Corbis
Contributing Editor: Jennifer Ceaser
Book Design: Michael DeLisio

No part of this publication may be reproduced in whole or in part, or stored in a retrieval system, or transmitted in any form or by any means, electronic, mechanical, photocopying, recording, or otherwise, without written permission of the publisher. For information regarding permission, write to Permissions Department, Grolier Incorporated, a subsidiary of Scholastic Inc., 90 Old Sherman Turnpike, Danbury, Connecticut 06816.

ISBN 0-516-24523-6

Copyright © 2000 by Rosen Book Works, Inc. All rights reserved. Published by Scholastic Inc., 557 Broadway, New York, NY 10012. SCHOLASTIC and associated logos are trademarks and/or registered trademarks of Scholastic Inc.

25 24 23 22 18 19/0

Printed in China. 62

First Scholastic printing, September 2002

Scholastic Inc., 557 Broadway, New York, NY 10012.

Contents

1	At the Police Station	6
2	Writing a Ticket	8
3	Patroling on Horses	10
4	Working With Buster	18
5	New Words	22
6	To Find Out More	23
7	Index	24
8	About the Author	24

We are **police officers**.

We help people.

We keep people safe.

We start our day at the **police station**.

We find out where we will **patrol** that day.

CRIME INFORMATION
REWARD

I patrol the roads.

I make sure people don't break the **law**.

I have to write a **ticket** if a person drives too fast.

POLICE
DEPARTMENT
CITY OF NEW YORK
9

We patrol on horses.

There's a big **parade** today.

We make sure that people march safely.

POLICE
15032

I patrol on a boat.

I make sure that everyone is being safe in the water.

POLICE
13

I patrol on a bike.

I ride my bike through the park.

I make sure everyone in the park is safe.

POLICE
NYPD
FUJI

I work in the street.

I use my hands to tell cars when to stop and go.

I make sure people cross the street safely.

POLICE

I patrol with Buster.

Buster is a police dog.

Buster helps me look for **clues**.

B.C.S.O.
K9

Sometimes I stop and talk to people.

They thank me for keeping them safe.

I'm happy to help them.

POLICE
DEPARTMENT
CITY OF NEW YORK

New Words

clues (klooz) things that help police figure out when someone has done something wrong

law (law) a rule that people must follow

parade (puh-**rayd**) a group of people that march together down a street

patrol (puh-**trol**) to keep a place safe

police officers (puh-**leese aw**-fih-sirz) people who make sure others are safe and follow laws

police station (puh-**leese stay**-shen) a place where police officers work

ticket (**tik**-it) something given to a driver who breaks the law

To Find Out More

Books

Officer Brown Keeps Neighborhoods Safe
by Alice K. Flanagan
Children's Press

Web Site

Super Trooper
http://www.users.fast.net/~louis2/index.html
This site has information about police officers and the equipment they use. It also includes important safety tips.

Index

bike, 14
boat, 12

clues, 18

horses, 10

law, 8

parade, 10
park, 14
patrol, 6, 8, 10, 12, 14, 18

police dog, 18
police station, 6

ticket, 8

About the Author

Jan Kottke is the owner/director of several preschools in the Tidewater area of Virginia. A lifelong early education professional, she is completing a phonics reading series for preschoolers.

Reading Consultants

Kris Flynn, Coordinator, Small School District Literacy, The San Diego County Office of Education

Shelly Forys, Certified Reading Recovery Specialist, W.J. Zahnow Elementary School, Waterloo, IL

Peggy McNamara, Professor, Bank Street College of Education, Reading and Literacy Program